# POCKET FULL OF HAPPINESS

## *WISDOM FOR A HAPPIER LIFE*

*SHANNON HORTON*

ISBN 978-1-7324431-0-5

Happinessmattersllc.com

# Dedication

Mike and Chloe you have been enormous support for my dreams. I love you both!

Thank you to all my family, friends and clients for your unending love and support of my dreams! Thank you Jenny for inspiring the book title!

# How to Use This Book

This book is a collection of my "Thought of the Day" posts of inspiring information, thoughts and questions to create a happier life.  You can read the book from front to cover. You can read a different page every day or you can even randomly open the book for your message of the day.

My wish is that this book inspires seeds of happy change to thrive in all areas of your life!

# TABLE OF CONTENTS

# CHAPTER 1
# WHAT IS HAPPINESS?

Happiness is your soul flying free in who it is.

-Shannon Horton

Happiness is a choice. You can choose to be happy or let a situation, person or event rule your mind and emotional space.

-Shannon Horton

Do more of which makes your heart sing the songs of happiness.

-Shannon Horton

Happiness is never external validation. It's an internal knowing you are valued, loved and accepted just for being you.

-Shannon Horton

"True happiness is not attained through self-gratification, but through fidelity to a worthy purpose".

-Helen Keller

What is your purpose to fulfill in life? Identifying the "what" is the first step.

-Shannon Horton

Your calling to serve in your own unique way is a sure path to happiness. Is it really worth holding back and hiding from pursuing this in the name of FEAR?

-Shannon Horton

## What is Happiness?

Happiness Matters definition of *happiness is:*

*As a spiritual being, when we are holistically aligned with our mental, emotional and physical values, we are in our natural state of happiness which propels us to continuously grow and create with the highest importance and without compromising our values.*

*-Shannon Horton*

## What is Happiness?

"Happiness is when what you think, what you say, and what you do, are in harmony."

-Mahatma Ghandi

Are your thoughts, words and actions in alignment with your heart? Are you speaking what you mean?

Are you taking action with a happy heart?

-Shannon Horton

## What is Happiness?

"The foolish man seeks happiness in the distance, the wise grows it under his feet".

- James Oppenheim

Be present today and what are you grateful for right now in your life? This helps you to remember there is happiness right now in your life. Sometimes, we have to look harder for the happiness versus the unhappiness.

-Shannon Horton

# CHAPTER 2
# THOUGHTS AND HAPPINESS

It is simple math; unhealthy thoughts, actions and feelings will never equal a happy and fulfilled life.

-Shannon Horton

Your external world is a direct reflection of your internal world.

-Shannon Horton

If every thought manifested immediately, would you think it? Think the thoughts that matter!

-Shannon Horton

# One bad moment is not worth giving it a whole day.

-Shannon Horton

Pay attention to
your feeling space.
It will show you
where your
thoughts are.

-Shannon Horton

Live now! Be happy now! Change your perception to see the truth versus the wounded filter you see life through.

-Shannon Horton

What took away
your childlike
happiness?

Is it worth that
much power?

-Shannon Horton

If you always look for the bad, you will see more bad. However, it is also true if you always look for the good; you will see more good.

-Shannon Horton

Your brain cannot tell the difference between actual or remembered experience or thoughts for yourself or another. You experience everything you think. Consciousness, however, travels towards others.

-Shannon Horton

You always have a choice. Making no choice is still a choice.

-Shannon Horton

What would happen if you saw life through the eyes of love and forgiveness?

-Shannon Horton

You draw into your life what you focus on.

-Shannon Horton

Meeting a problem with the same thinking and energy will never heal the problem. Rise above with a higher vibration; love.

-Shannon Horton

Watch how the vibrations of lack creep into your thoughts or words such as “it's too expensive, I can't afford it”. Change these thoughts to “that's affordable or I can afford, however, choose to wait”.

-Shannon Horton

Your opinion of yourself is the only one that matters.

-Shannon Horton

How have the unhealthy emotions and thoughts been working for you?

Have they manifested what you want?

-Shannon Horton

Focusing on problems or debt just gives you more problems or debt. Focus it's already resolved or gone and it will be.

-Shannon Horton

You have everything to gain by changing your unhealthy mindset to healthier mindset.

-Shannon Horton

Don't be afraid to go where you've never gone and do what you've never done, because both are necessary to have what you've never had and be who you've never been.

-The Universe (TUT Messages by Mike Dooley)

The Universe rewards us when we take a leap of faith with a peaceful heart!

-Shannon Horton

Our egos only understand the logic it was given. Sometimes, a higher intelligence perspective is hard to understand. Today, trust that for whatever reason, things are still working out in your favor even if it appears they are not.

Key word: TRUST.

-Shannon Horton

Everything in your life was created by your thoughts and the emotions you have been feeling in response to those thoughts.

- Shannon Horton

# Thoughts and Happiness

Just because you have a thought, does not mean it is true.

What unhealthy thoughts are you thinking about yourself and your life? Are those what you want to believe?

Change them to the things you want to believe about yourself. If these thoughts make you feel heavy and not good about yourself, they are not a truth. They are not in alignment with you. Thoughts that give you lightness and peace are. Pay attention and stop giving unhealthy thoughts any power or time!

-Shannon Horton

Remember, you are an amazing and powerful being! You have the power to change your life through your emotions and thoughts. What do you want to create? Focus your thoughts and emotions to having created it!

-Shannon Horton

Judgment gets in the way of miracles. Do not judge how big or small something is. Sometimes, it's the smallest of the changes or events that lead to the biggest opportunities and manifestations!

Just observe and follow the signs that are guiding you to your desired outcome.

-Shannon Horton

There are only two ways to live your life. One is as though nothing is a miracle. The other is as though everything is a miracle.

- Albert Einstein

I am choosing "everything" is a miracle. How about you?

Take a day off from your "problems" mentally and emotionally! Allow yourself to feel free as if they are already resolved! See what happens. You might have a huge surprise!

-Shannon Horton

## THOUGHTS AND HAPPINESS

Where is the tension in your life? What are your thoughts and emotions around that situation?

What if you looked at it differently? What if you came from a more loving perspective?

Do you think it would change? Obviously, how you are responding and thinking toward it isn't working on resolving it. Try a new path!

-Shannon Horton

What makes your heart sing? What are you waiting for in pursuing it? If you are waiting for it to "all line up", you may never do it!

Sometimes it is taking the first leap of faith to move the energy in action! You are unlimited in your potential!!! Reach for the Stars!!

-Shannon Horton

Check in. Look at your life.

What area could you change to increase your success and happiness?

-Shannon Horton

Perceptions are often misleading. They come from places where we hold fear, trauma and unhealthy stories about ourselves, others and the world. Where do your perceptions need to shift to see the "truth"?

-Shannon Horton

What if thinking and focusing on the "problems" in your life are actually keeping them from being solved? What if you keep your thoughts and energy to the place that all is already solved? Change your thoughts to 95% of the time on things being resolved and what you want and only 5% of the time dealing with the "problems".

Try it! See how those things start resolving on their own almost by magic through opportunities, blessings and even just "disappearing" on their own. This magic is called a miracle! They are more common than you think. -Shannon Horton

"Your "problem" does not define you. It is a map to what your consciousness is focusing on".

-Dr. Wayne Dyer – (Change your thoughts-Change your life)

Your job, level of wealth and hobbies are not who you are just as your problems are not a reflection of who you are. They are just a reflection of where your energy is being given. The big question is: What are the qualities of your soul?

-Shannon Horton

Think of all your accomplishments; great and small. They matter! You are who you are today because of them and show the immense courage you do have!

-Shannon Horton

Living in the past only keeps you in the past unless you bring the blessings, lessons, knowledge and insights to the present.

What skills or talents from your past are calling you to nurture and use to improve your life?

Are there any old "dreams" calling you to revisit them once again?

-Shannon Horton

Thoughts, beliefs and words have the power to create or destroy your goals, desires and wishes. Be careful what you put out there. If every thought came true instantly, would you think them?

-Shannon Horton

The thoughts you think about other people are actually the stories you believe about yourself. Change the story you think of yourself and others and your life will transform!

-Shannon Horton

"Man can form things in his thought, and, by impressing his thought upon formless substance, can cause the thing he thinks about to be created".

-Wallace Wattles

Our thoughts are powerful. The thoughts that create human emotion are the most powerful.  Align your desires with your feeling of having it now. This is the key to manifestation.

-Shannon Horton

Which do you choose?

"Beliefs have the power to create and the power to destroy"

-Tony Robbins

## Thoughts and Happiness

"When I let go of what I am, I become what I might be"

-Lao Tzu.

Attachment and judgment to who we are and what we are expected to be/do can be a block to happiness. Instead of fully planning your next steps, have flexibility and allow the steps and aspects of your divine nature come through and reveal themselves to you. Miracles reveal themselves in the most amazing way!

-Shannon Horton

"Our belief system is based off our evaluation of something. Often, if we re-evaluate it, our belief will change"

-Bob Proctor

Ask the divine to see the truth in all situations and circumstances. What you ask for is given. It may not be what your ego perceives.

-Shannon Horton

Whatever the mind believes, it can achieve.
Overcome the limitations within yourself to achieve your dreams!

-Shannon Horton

"It isn't what happens that matters. It is the meaning we give it that matters".

-Joe Vitale

It is the unhealthy perspective we attach to an event that creates more pain and suffering. Choose to see the blessing in everything because everything does work in your favor!

-Shannon Horton

Today, focus on what is important. If the list gets done it gets done. Peace and being able to be present for the gifts that are appearing before you now is what matters. That to do list can be a distraction from what we want but are afraid to grasp hold of! Enjoy the day and watch you miraculously achieve what is important with ease!

-Shannon Horton

What if all the fears you have are only powerful because you give them the energy of your mind? What if they are trying to fool you from recognizing and living your full potential? How would you change this if you knew this was true?

-Shannon Horton

Judgments and unhealthy beliefs cause us to spiral down the toxic thought and emotion rabbit hole. Instead step back and say "Isn't this interesting?" Allow your inner observer see the "truth" versus "your perception". There is a blessing and growth opportunity in everything.

-Shannon Horton

# CHAPTER 3
# ALL ABOUT THE VIBRATION

"Vibration creates geometry and geometry creates matter. Therefore, our feelings create our reality".

-David Wilcock

What part of your life do you not like? Then change your thoughts and feelings to match what it is you want.

-Shannon Horton

"Too many of us are not living our dreams because we are living our fears".

-Les Brown

Are you living your dreams? What will you regret more, following your dreams or holding back from living your dreams? Having regret is heavier on the heart than discovering you are amazingly capable of creating your dreams.

-Shannon Horton

# Fear instantly stops your manifestation.

-Shannon Horton

Feel as if you have your "what" now and hold for a minimum of 1 minute each day.

The universe will start to immediately bring the how to you.

-Shannon Horton

# It's a minute too long to live an unloved and unhappy life.

-Shannon Horton

What would your ideal life look like? Now feel what that would feel like to have it now!!

-Shannon Horton

The great illusion is that life happens to us. The truth is we create our life and reality.

-Shannon Horton

If it feels heavy, it's not in alignment with you.

If it feels light, it is in alignment.

-Shannon Horton

A miraculous life is being in loving control of your vibrational feeling space. Miracles then happen all the time.

-Shannon Horton

Thought without feeling is powerful but thought that activates intense feeling is the most powerful creator of reality and influencer of matter.

-Shannon Horton

"All the solutions exist before a problem was ever thought of or recognized".

-Richard Dotts

How would your life look if you lived your life as if all the solutions exist and appear as you need them? How would your life look if you lived life as if everything works in your favor always?

-Shannon Horton

Lack mindset will
always make you
feel heavy.
Abundance will
always feel light.

-Shannon Horton

Waiting to be the vibration of having your goal will always keep you waiting for your goal.

-Shannon Horton

# 'Being' which is feeling the vibration of having your goal now manifests your goal into the now.

-Shannon Horton

# Has worrying resolved the issue? Then why worry???

-Shannon Horton

What do you want to create in your life? Now stop and reflect if your daily thoughts are in alignment with that desire? If they are not, change them to be! Hold the thoughts and vibration it already is and it will be!!

-Shannon Horton

Love is the most powerful force in the Universe and can create miracles. How can you be more loving toward yourself and others today?

–Shannon Horton

What attachment can you let go of today and just surrender to know that your outcome will be just as it is supposed to be? Feel the end result of 'the what' and hold that vibration instead of being attached to the 'hows'.

–Shannon Horton

Time to do that thing you have wanted to try or do for a long time! Feel and see yourself doing it and see how the opportunities align for you to do it. It is time to let go of all excuses of 'why not' and find reasons 'why you can'.

–Shannon Horton

Today, right now, is a great time to start loving your life! You created it!

–Shannon Horton

What dreams do you want to manifest? Spend 5 minutes today feeling the dream is there in your life! How does that feel??

Let's give energy to that we love versus what we don't!!!

–Shannon Horton

You are the factor that allows your life to be in the perfect flow or not. Which do you choose?

–Shannon Horton

## All About The Vibration

Faith is the major foundation of any manifestation! You only have control of how you participate in the world; actions, thoughts, words, feeling, not how the world participates around you. Have faith that all will manifest perfectly and your desires and dreams may manifest more miraculous than you ever imagined!

-Shannon Horton

Energy always tells the truth. Please make sure your words are aligning with your energy. People can tell when there is a discrepancy.

-Shannon Horton

What are you giving your power to today? Is it worth your energy? If not, SHIFT it to what is!!

-Shannon Horton

You are more amazing and beautiful than you imagine!

- Shannon Horton

"Fear only exists when you do not understand that you have the power to project thought and that the Universe will respond".

-Abraham Hicks

Live in the moment. Be present and trust that all you need and desire is on its way to you. Don't give up before your manifestation has appeared.

-Shannon Horton

Your love is your greatest power! Allow yourself to be that love and watch miracles happen in your life!

- Shannon Horton

Courage is faith that no matter the outcome, everything works out in your favor.

- Shannon Horton

If all you felt was love for yourself, your life and the world, how would your life look and feel? Love is the most powerful force in the Universe! Make it your super power!

- Shannon Horton

There are infinite solutions and possibilities just as there are infinite unique snowflakes.

- Shannon Horton

# Everything you seek is SEEKING YOU!

Most of us have the system of creating backwards. We believe the paradigm of 'Have-Do-Be'. However, it is 'BE-DO-HAVE'. We have to be the vibration, thoughts and actions of the goal we desire, then act upon and participate in the opportunities that come our way to lead us to HAVE it! Start changing your mind set to this and miracles will unfold!

- Shannon Horton

Learning to control your thoughts that create emotional reactions that create your "state of being" is very important!! It is this combination; thoughts and emotional images create the reality around you. All it takes is one healthy change you do daily for a month to start changing your stress and reality. Keep this change going and add a new healthy change each month. After a year, you have made 12 healthy changes that are now habits.

- Shannon Horton

## ALL ABOUT THE VIBRATION

This is a reminder to check in where your mind is today. What are you putting your energy on? Are your thoughts aligning with what you want to create? If not, time to step back and reframe your mind to look at things differently. Vibrate at the level of what you want to create in your life. Think thoughts that make you happy. Reach out to your like-minded friends for support. Stop and get an ice cream. Participate in those activities that return to you to your beautiful state of mind.

- Shannon Horton

## ALL ABOUT THE VIBRATION

Actualize your greatness, your potential, your light within to create the image of the life you really want! Where are you settling out of fear for much less than the life you want? When you look at this aspect of your life, what is the first thing you can do to change it? It may mean just making the commitment to change it and face each fear with confidence that those steps lead to amazing new paths of happiness and fulfillment. You have a choice to stay in the old that keeps getting you the old or changing your approach by facing those fears and taking your power back!

- Shannon Horton

## All About The Vibration

We control the law of attraction through our vibration. What level are you vibrating at? Are amazing things happening or are there more frustrating things happening?

Change your vibration by changing your perception. Thinking 'isn't that interesting' takes us out of judgment and into observing. Feel 'everything always works out for me'. If you believe it, it does!

- Shannon Horton

# CHAPTER 4

## IT IS SCIENCE

Smile all the time. Your brain will respond with happiness.

- Shannon Horton

People are not their behavior. Behavior is a learned response for safety, security and to get needs met. It comes from the 0 to 6 year old unconscious child the majority of the time.

- Shannon Horton

The unconscious mind is 1000 more powerful than the conscious mind. Use your feeling space well.

It takes only a minute of holding your feeling space on your intention to start activating the field to start bringing it to you.

Hippocrates said "All disease begins in the gut". What healthy diet change can you make today that will improve your health and wellbeing?

Remember, it is a lifestyle change not a fad.

- Shannon Horton

## It Is Science

It's easier to remember all the unhealthy events that happen to us because our brains are designed to keep us alert to danger. However, it is often an inaccurate perception of reality. Think of 10 events in your life that were amazing. Start training your mind to focus on the healthy experiences versus the unhealthy.

- Shannon Horton

It is estimated that 1/3 of all healings are unrelated to medicine or treatment. It is from the belief it will work and they will get better!

-Dr. Bruce Lipton

Your mind is powerful! Your mind and feeling together are extremely powerful!

-Shannon Horton

"No man is wise enough by himself"

- Plautus

Remember, one of the biggest keys to happiness is the depth of our social relationships and through them, we grow.

-Shannon Horton

## It Is Science

Did you know that "LOVE" can restart the heart? It can.

Did you know that you can die of a broken heart? Yes, you can.

If love can restart the heart, let's live being that love daily to the world. Think of how powerful that can be to restart the heart of the world!!

Peace is possible.

Love your own life first and spread that love outward!

## It Is Science

Only 25% of our success is based on Intelligence and technical skills combined. 75% of our success is based on four things. Our optimism; how we perceive life. The belief that our behavior matters when faced with challenge. Our social interaction and connection; the depth and meaning of our relationships which is directly connected to our happiness. Our view of stress; if we view stress as a challenge, our brains turn on to the highest possible level. If we view stress as a threat, it shuts off the brain into fight or flight response that resists the very things that help us achieve our potential.

-Based on the research of Shawn Achor

We are all connected to everyone in the world by 6 degrees or steps. It is a small world with big possibilities. We are truly connected to each other. Be kind to each other!

# It Is Science

We have over 60,000 thoughts a day and over for most people 80% of them are negative or unhealthy. The Subconscious/unconscious mind is 1000 times more powerful than the conscious mind and fighting for control. 95% of our behaviors are controlled by subconscious beliefs. Our experiences do not define us. It is who we learn to be. Change the subconscious beliefs and our lives will change!

Maladaptive Stress Reaction is when a situation, thought or experience triggers an unconscious belief or trauma and the body believes that it is happening again. Our thoughts and emotions react to the pictures/memories attached to them. Emotions and memories are the root of every symptom, disease and stress. These emotions, memories and traumatic perceptions are hidden in the subconscious mind.

The removal of stress creates health. The AMA states that 80% of all health related issue are stress related!!!

Where can you let go of the stress? Do you have to change your job? If you put your needs first, would this reduce your stress? Having a hobby?

SAY NO TO STRESS and YES to YOU!

## It Is Science

Remember, the only person we can control is ourselves. We can control the stories and judgments we have about others, situations and ourselves before they take over. We can control how we act and react to life around us. Remember, 90 % of our happiness is based on how we perceive and interact with the external world around us! If your external world is chaotic, stressful and unhappy look within. This is where an adjustment in the thoughts, actions and beliefs is necessary to start creating an external world you truly desire!

The external world accounts for only 10% of our happiness.

Our thoughts directly link to our health. Scientists are proving that the way we think and feel have a direct effect on our health and wellbeing. "75% to 95% of the illnesses that plague us today are a direct result of our thought life" (Dr. Leaf, 2016). Want to improve your health? Forgive others and yourself, let go of the past and all the unhealthy thoughts and emotions. Instead focus your energy on what you want to feel and think instead of allowing your brain to spiral out of control with the same unhealthy thinking pattern!

Being happier is important to health and wellbeing! It can reduce one's chances of heart disease by 30%. The mind/body connection is real and important to address!!

How many smiles can you give to others or yourself today?

The moment you smile, the happiness neurotransmitter dopamine releases. Be the smile that makes a difference today for someone! Plus, you feel the happiness benefit first!

Do you know that we are
wirelessly connected to
others through our mirror
neurons in the brain and
sensory-neurites in the
heart? Did you know that by
doing one positive change in
how you view the world
around you, that you help
change the ones around you?

The U.S. Air Force proved the energetic field that connects all life exists in 1987. Science has proven our thoughts and emotions create our reality by activating this field to bring the desire to us.

Where the mind goes, the body follows.

Your body instantly feels the thoughts and emotions you have.

The brain absorbs 20% of all nutrients ingested.

It is 10 times more metabolically active than the body. Eat a healthy diet in good fat, protein and foods.

# CHAPTER 5
# TAKE ACTION

Accountability for our participation gives us the ability to change our circumstances. Blaming keeps us a victim.

- Shannon Horton

The Beatles understood happiness.

Just 'Let it Be'.

- Shannon Horton

Ten deep breaths reset and center the brain and nervous system.

Make use of this amazing tool!

- Shannon Horton

# Tap your way to happiness.

## Use EFT (Emotional Freedom Technique) to reduce unhealthy thoughts and emotions.

- Shannon Horton

# Balance your brain and emotions with Binaural beats music.

Binaural Beats Meditation

https://www.binauralbeatsmeditation.com/?ap_id=Shannon

Practicing breath work before holding the intention and vibration of what you would like to create magnifies your intention vibration 10 fold.

-Shannon Horton

Go back to focusing on serving. Trust the rest is already falling into and is in place!

- Shannon Horton

You are magnificent!

You deserve and the universe has unlimited opportunities to get you where your heart wants to be.

- Shannon Horton

## Ask the right questions. The universe sends the answers.

Higher questions:

What is the blessing?

What can I do to serve?

Where are my skills and talents needed?

What can I do now to shift my awareness?

What is the learning experience?

- Shannon Horton

There is a blessing and opportunity in everything. It's your choice to ask it to reveal itself.

- Shannon Horton

You are what you surround yourself with. Be careful to what you let into your mind and personal space.

Environment is stronger than will.

- Shannon Horton

There is no such thing as coincidence; there is only synchronicity.

The universe doesn't waste it’s time to send you on a wild goose chase. Pay attention to the signs it's showing you. Its mission is to help you thrive and succeed.

- Shannon Horton

Every day is a new canvas. What will you create today?

- Shannon Horton

# You matter or else God wouldn't have sent you on this mission.

- Shannon Horton

We are all beautiful
and loving beings.
Remember, to focus on
that and always treat
others with love and
respect. Including
listening with the
intention to listen.

- Shannon Horton

A miraculous life is being in loving control of your vibrational feeling space. Miracles then happen all the time.

- Shannon Horton

Always rise to do the right thing. Peace is the reward.

- Shannon Horton

Life is too short to live on the sidelines.

Life is a dance. Enjoy it!

- Shannon Horton

"Choose a job you love and you will never have to work a day in your life".

- Confucius

Life is far too short and precious to work a job you dislike. You have special talents and gifts for a reason! Find your purpose and live your calling in life!

-Shannon Horton

## Take Action

"Never forget that if there weren't any need for you in all your uniqueness to be on this earth, you wouldn't be here in the first place" –

Dr. Wayne W. Dyer,

I Can See Clearly Now

It is society's fear of the uniqueness in each of us that programs us to hide our light.  We are designed to shine our light.  That is the natural essence of who we are. Unhappiness comes from dimming the love and light within us.

-Shannon Horton

What have you been too busy to do for you? Take time to schedule in those things and activities you need to rejuvenate yourself.

Only you can control your schedule. Don't let your schedule control you! This is part of being fulfilled and happy.

- Shannon Horton

## TAKE ACTION

"Let go of the people who dull your shine, poison your spirit, and bring you drama. Cancel your subscription to their issues."
- Steve Maraboli, Speaker & Author

Surround yourself with like-minded people and situations to life your spirits and that fill you with joy! Drama and unhealthy interactions take too much of your life force away from what you desire to create in your life. See these unhealthy people and situations as happy, healthy and fulfilled. This is the biggest blessing you can give them.

-Shannon Horton

Do one random act of kindness today. Then watch how your world transforms!

-Shannon Horton

Today's challenge: Trust that the Universe is on your side all day! Everything works in your favor! Can you do it?? I BELIEVE YOU CAN!

-Shannon Horton

Take time for you today! Relax and breathe! Being too busy can hinder manifesting happiness just as much as fear does.

-Shannon Horton

## TAKE ACTION

Take time to be grateful for all your blessings! No matter how smoothly or rough your perception of your life is right now, gratitude will always shift things to be better! You will see all the blessings you have!

-Shannon Horton

## Take Action

What is your calling? Are you holding yourself back in an unhealthy or unhappy job waiting for everything aligning up perfectly to move to a calling? Maybe the Universal forces are waiting for the moment for you to decide that your calling is now before the first opportunity arises...It's up to you to decide to make it happen and then believe and feel it happening. Take the first step of faith to make your calling come true! Your thoughts and emotions are powerful creators of your life!

-Shannon Horton

## Take Action

Do you schedule fun in your day daily? Do you intend to have joy in everything you do? It's up to you what you get out of life. It's up to you if you do something fun every day and it's up to you if you have joy in everything you do. Change your perception and mindset and change your life!

-Shannon Horton

The inner light will always illuminate a darkened outer path.

-Shannon Horton

## TAKE ACTION

"You can observe a lot just by watching"

- Yogi Berra

Can you just be an observer today of all interactions including your own?

You may be surprised the insights, wisdom and areas to change your thinking that are revealed.

-Shannon Horton

## Take Action

Be Present! There is peace and happiness being with the moment you are in. Again, forget the "problems" that appear to be real and trust the solution will find you as soon as you let go!

How does it feel having the solution?

We often miss out on so much joy because we allow the stresses of life to consume us. Why? Focusing on the stress only causes more stress.

-Shannon Horton

## TAKE ACTION

Two week challenge:

All solutions exist even before a problem appears. Live your life as if the solutions are already there. Let go of the thoughts, words and worries. Hold the vibration of what it feels like to have your life perfectly flowing, all things resolved. Check in all day and where is your vibration?

Keep a journal of all the miracles that take place in detail.

-Shannon Horton

## Take Action

What resistance is appearing in your life in taking action for your dreams? Resistance means you are fearful going outside of your comfort zone. Comfort zones do not create growth, risk does!

Commit to taking action daily towards your dream even if that fear, doubt and insecurity is talking you out of it. You will see that action creates results and you will have less resistance.

-Shannon Horton

MAINFESTATION SECRET: Hold the "Vibration" of what you want to manifest in life. See the end result and FEEL what it looks like and feels like.

Let go of words. Check in every hour. Where is your vibration at? The longer you hold the vibration, the faster the Universe conspires to make it happen. Remember, it is about vibration.

FEEL your desire as if it is already there!

-Shannon Horton

Ask for divine guidance to see the truth versus your perception today and watch the miracles that happen. Often, it is only the way we see something that has to change in order for the situation to change.

-Shannon Horton

What opportunities will you look back on and regret not taking?

That is a clue to take a leap of faith! The Universe loves quick action.

-Shannon Horton

It is only when a comfort zone becomes uncomfortable and painful enough, that it is less painful and fearful to leap off the ledge and discover we can fly.

-Shannon Horton

Healthy risk is a good thing! You realize you are more powerful than you have made yourself believe!

-Shannon Horton

Your life is rich with resources and opportunity!

-Shannon Horton

What is one step you can do today that brings you closer to your dreams and your true self? Now do it!

-Shannon Horton

"Today I will Speak from the Heart" - Marianne Williamson, 2013

Speaking truth from the heart with love is received with love and with the heart. Our words we think and speak are reflected in the life we are experiencing. If our life isn't quite what we want; change the words you think and speak in.

-Shannon Horton

"Let integrity and uprightness distinguish all your acts” and "Be generous in prosperity. Be thankful in adversity" - Baha'u'llah

Let the way you live your life be the inspiration to others!

Reflect: If I died today, would I be proud in the way I lived my life? Would I be proud of the legacy I leave behind?

If not, make a commitment to be the change in your own life that you want to see. Remember, the how is not as important and the "what and why". After knowing those, the "how" appears.

-Shannon Horton

## Take Action

Is there a person or are here persons that have impacted your life and you never told them how and thank you?

Today, write a letter, email or text to tell them how that moment impacted you and your life. You never know how that can lift a person up knowing they made a difference.

What a gift it is to that person and yourself by expressing that impactful moment or story and giving recognition to that soul that helped you along the way!

-Shannon Horton

## TAKE ACTION

We have hundreds of habits we do daily. Some are healthy, others may be unhealthy. Take a moment to discover your habits. Ask that the top unhealthy habits be revealed to you. They could be diet, they could be "sabotaging" habits, and they could be language habits. Whatever they are, be open to the unhealthy habits that reveal themselves to you and what "healthy" habit would you like to replace them with? Then commit to making that healthy habit a habit.

-Shannon Horton

## Take Action

Many times the biggest leaps we make in life are when we have faith and knowing that we need to do something. We are not waiting for everything to align up perfectly. It is when we take the leap "not" knowing how it will work out, the money and opportunity will appear.

If you have an idea, a calling, a desire; take that leap of faith! Commit to your desire, have unwavering faith and don't worry about the "how". It will show itself! That is the amazing part of the journey!

-Shannon Horton

## Take Action

What will it take for you to love your life?

When you reflect on your life now, is everything awesome?

Do you have one or two areas that you struggle to love?
Remember, to love is a choice. We can learn to love those difficult situations and people just as we love the awesome situations and people. Learning to love the "difficult" actually expands our capability to love ourselves and change our reality profoundly.

BE THE LOVE YOU WANT TO EXPERIENCE IN YOUR LIFE!

-Shannon Horton

# Take Action

Happiness is a choice!

When you choose to invest in your happiness miracles happen! Choose to expand your awareness. Ask how, what, where and why questions instead of accepting your perception of your reality as real.

Example: How can I make this happen? That is the difference between a resourceful person and an unresourceful person's thinking.

"It is the lack of resourcefulness not resources that results in failure" (Tony Robbins, 2016).

-Shannon Horton

# About the Author

Shannon has a Masters in Professional Counseling from GCU. Her undergraduate degrees are in Holistic Healthcare (from SWIHA) and Complementary and Alternative Healthcare (from Ashford University). She is a Psychic Intuitive Medium and Motivational Speaker.

She is passionate about holistic healing and helping her clients thrive through her Intuitive Coaching Sessions, Happiness and Wellness coaching, Public Speaking and workshops.

## ABOUT HAPPINESS MATTERS, LLC

Happiness Matters is a unique business providing workshops to corporations, businesses, schools and organizations on the science of 'Happiness' and related topics.

For more information:

Happiness Matters, LLC

Shannon@happinessmattersllc.com

www.happinessmattersllc.com

Happiness Matters

Made in the USA
Las Vegas, NV
06 December 2023

82220447R00100